C000174031

ANYTHING IS
(POSSIBLY)
POSSIBLE

KNOCK
KNOCK®
VENICE, CALIFORNIA

Created, published, and distributed by Knock Knock
1635 Electric Ave.
Venice, CA 90291
knockknockstuff.com
Knock Knock is a registered trademark of
Knock Knock LLC

Design by Office of Paul Sahre

ISBN: 978-168349082-1
UPC: 825703-50178-0

10 9 8 7 6 5 4 3 2 1

Motivational speakers and theoretical physicists tell us that anything is possible. They tell us that our reality is only limited by our imagination. But guess what? Most of us weren't raised that way. And even if we were, it's still hard for anyone to feel infinitely powerful when facing rush-hour traffic, online trolls, or paper cuts. That's what this book is for. Consider it your own little pocket pep talk. Open it up whenever you need to be reminded that you are a being of infinite potential, or when your delusions of grandeur need a tune-up.

So get out there and go for it. Or take a nap and try again tomorrow.

I am neither an optimist nor pessimist, but a possibilist.

Max Lerner

The world has told
you lies about how
small you are, but a
possibilist.

Heather Havrilesky

Fdwelhinfapos

Emily Dickinson

bilitybrave.

You've got to build
a house
because you're going
to live in it. It's
terribly important
that the doors to
your room, yourself,
are not closed. And
that you keep saying,
"Yes! Yes! Why not?"
comet, any planet.

Katharine Hepburn

Once I got into
space, I was feeling
very comfortable in
the universe. I felt
like I had a right to
be anywhere in this
universe, that I
belonged here as
much as any speck
of stardust, any
comet, any planet.

Mae Jemison

The world is
filled with all
opportunities—
so grow the
tension of waiting
to be struck.

Maya Angelou

The world is all gates, all opportunities— strings of tension waiting to be struck.

Ralph Waldo Emerson

We each experience of my life, I have had to step out of one little space of the known light, into a large area of darkness. I had to stand awhile in the darkness, and then gradually God has given me light. But not to rest in. For as soon as that light has felt familiar, then the call has always come to step out ahead again into new darkness.

Mary McLeod Bethune

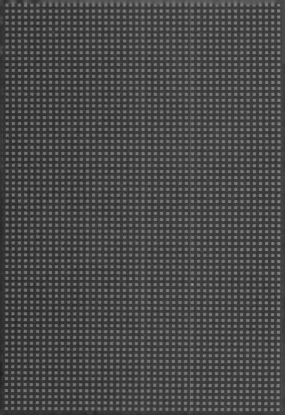

We are part of this of my
Universe; we are in this
Universe, but perhaps of
more important than a
both of those facts, is
that the Universe is in
us. When I reflect then
that fact, I look up given
many people feel small,
'cause they're small and
the Universe is big, but
I feel big, because my
atoms came from to step
those stars. again into
new darkness.

Neil deGrasse Tyson

Big eats my own body to
Look at my own and
recognize, so fragile, so
With eyes kill no longer
easy to kill.
blind—
Don't forget that,
And of see that don't own
All I see that my own
hands can make
with them.

The world that's in
my mind.

Langston Hughes

Big ideas are so hard to
recognize, so fragile, so
easy to kill...
Don't forget that,
All of you who don't own
them... make

The world that's in
my mind.

Soldiers are no longer
With eyes no longer
blind—
All of you that don't
have them.

John Elliott, Jr.

Anything is possible. Stay
open, forever, so
open it hurts, and
then open up
some more, until
the day you die,
world without
end, amen.

George Saunders

She would be a
possible person, she
vowed. They said
no matter how
far a mule travels
it can never come
back a horse, but
she would show
them all.

Junot Díaz

Fortune favors the bold

Virgil

be little brave.

One day

You will happen / It will blossom

One day, one day

When you make / It will all make

sense / ready

One day

You will blossom
It will happen

One day, one day

When you're ready
I will make
ready

Björk

When I had asked
God for one, or two
extra inches in
height, but instead
he made me as tall
as the sky, so high
that I could not
measure myself.

Malala Yousafzai

Without leaps of
imagination, or
dreaming, we lose
the excitement
of possibilities.
Dreaming, after
all, is a form of
planning.

Gloria Steinem

That if we go down
into ourselves
we find that
we possess
exactly what
we desire.

Simone Weil

That is happiness; to
be dissolved into something
complete and great.

George Eliot

My comfort zone is like a little bubble, and I've pushed it in different directions and made it bigger, and bigger until these objectives that seemed totally crazy eventually fall within the realm of the possible.

Alex Honnold

At first people refuse to
believe that a strange
new thing can be done,
then they begin to
hope it can be done,
then they see it can be
done — then it is done
and all the world
wonders why it was
not done centuries ago.

Frances Hodgson Burnett

Life shrinks or expands in proportion to one's courage.

Anaïs Nin

We have been
raised to fear
the yes within
ourselves.

(overlaid with)

Welcome the
risk to learn
the power to
courage.

Audre Lorde

We aspecial

What I aim

Nannie Helen Burroughs

ze in the
ossible.

Passivity is
the dragon
that every
woman has to
murder in her
quest for
independence.

Jill Johnston

Imagination has always had powers of resurrection that no science can snatch.

independence.

Ingrid Bengis

If I were to wish for
something, I would
not wish for wealth
or power, but for
the passion of
possibility, for the
eye, eternally young,
eternally ardent,
that sees possibility
everywhere.

Søren Kierkegaard

There is a way to
hold onto something
that doesn't exist yet.
That's what takes
place when a song
is written. You see
something that isn't
there. Then you use
your instrument to
find it.

John Frusciante

Inspiration is
for amateurs —
the rest of us
just show up
and get to
work.

Chuck Close

It is our choices,
Harry, that
show what we
truly are, far
more than our
abilities.

J. K. Rowling

Integrate what you
believe into every
single area of your life.
Don't try to special,
character and values,
the secret that yourselves
know. It's okay if else
does, the definition is
don't let that get
swallowed up by the
great choking
complacency.

Meryl Streep

Self-definition and
self-determination is
about the audacity
and strength to proclaim,
create, and evolve into
who we know ourselves
to be. It's okay if your
personal definition is
in a constant state of
flux as you navigate
the world.

complacency.

Janet Mock

When you're / Men know what
the day after, / they want and
tomorrow will / everyone is
bring the very / thing but they
thing / this
want / and, you
haven't / keep doing
what / love!
to hope.

William Maxwell

When you're
disgusting, and
everyone is
grossed out by
you and thinks
you're gross, you
know, keep doing
what you love!
to hope.

Maria Bamford

Reasityci

Whaltyaico

Robin Williams

in the

ceptible.

Talent is insignificant.
I know a lot of talented
ruins. Beyond talent
lie all the usual words:
discipline, love, luck,
but, most of all,
endurance.

James Baldwin

I learned to stand up
for myself early on
because I learned that
if I didn't, nobody else
would do it for me.
You want something,
you do it yourself.

Loretta Young

My gift for fantasy
has meant more to
me than my talent
for absorbing
positive knowledge.

Albert Einstein

Why, sometimes I've believed as many as six impossible things before breakfast.

Lewis Carroll

There is no
force equal
to a woman,
determined
to rise.
hieroglyphs.

W. E. B. DuBois

Build your own pyramids, write your own hieroglyphs.

There is no force equal to a woman determined to rise.

Kendrick Lamar

chute.

Marina Keegan

You can't be that kid standing at the top of the waterslide, overthinking it. You have to go down the chute.

Tina Fey

If adventures will not befall a young lady in her own village, she must seek them abroad.

Jane Austen

Opportunities are usually disguised as hard work, so most people don't recognize them.

Adventures will not befall a lazy day home, so village people don't seek abroad.

Ann Landers

Hope is a

adventure

nothing

George Bernanos

æɪskghat

uɒr

t all.

Well, I can tell you... fear is just
part of it... making... fear,
that's a good thing, you
know? ...I often feel that...
So, at the very limits
of what I'm capable... you
fck. I feel like I has
actually sort of scared
all the time.

Ira Glass

What I realize is that fear, that's the worst of it. That's the real enemy. So, get up, get out in the real world and you kick that bastard as hard as you can right in the teeth.

Walter White (*Breaking Bad*)

A winner is
that person
who gets up
one more time.
Given up she
is knocked
down

Being defeated
is often a
temporary
condition.
Giving it up
is what makes it
permanent.

Mia Hamm

Being defeated
is often a
temporary
condition.
Giving up is
what makes it
permanent.

Marilyn vos Savant

No matter how well
you perform there's
always somebody of
intelligent opinion
who thinks it's lousy.

Dreams come true;
without that possibility,
nature would not
incite us to have them.

John Updike

No matter how well
you perform there's
always somebody of
intelligent opinion
who thinks it's lousy.

Laurence Olivier

"Whenever I go on a ride,
I'm always thinking of
what's wrong with the
thing and how it can be
improved."

Walt Disney

"...would like to see us
take hold of ourselves,
look at ourselves and
cease being afraid... the
first step."

Eleanor Roosevelt

"It is hard to be brave," said Piglet, sniffing slightly, "when you're only a Very Small Animal."

A. A. Milne

Take the first step in faith. You don't have to see the whole staircase, just take the first step.

Martin Luther King, Jr.

Just don't
give up trying
to do what
you really
want to do.

Ella Fitzgerald

Just never
give up trying
fiction
life — really revise.

It is never
too late
to work on what
you really
want to do.

Nancy Thayer

Life is either a daring adventure or nothing

Helen Keller

æiskghat
uor
t all.

I always focused on
positive self-talk for
myself. I swear it
seems futile most of
the time. If you're like,
"This isn't doing some-
anything" but if you
stick with it, it really
does sink in and And
infiltrates your thing
subconscious and
stays there.

April Ross

The first secret to success is asking for yourself, what is it that is closest to my heart? If you fall in love with doing something, it means you'll stick with it actually and you'll do it a lot. And if you do something a lot you get really good at it.

Dr. S. James Gates, Jr.

If one always looked at the skies, one would end up with wings.

Gustave Flaubert

An invasion of
armies can be
resisted, but not
an idea whose
time has come.

Victor Hugo

Impossible is potential.
Impossible is temporary.
Impossible is **nothing**.
can hold me down.

Muhammad Ali

What is impossible is potential.
What is possible is temporary.
What is possible is **nothing**.
can hold me down.

Roxane Gay

"I found a new way the other day. It was like, Shit, if I had known that years ago. That's what's beautiful about the guitar. You think you know it all, and you keep on, and there's always something new to do to get better.

Keith Richards

"Finish each day and
be done with it. ... it was
like a shit, if I had
known that years
ago. That's what's
beautiful about the
guitar. Whatever you
messed up on today.
You have another
chance to get better.

Claressa Shields

Take up the be

Take it up. vict

It's wrong. Thi

This is your. w

Maya Angelou

ve. of a

y. You can't

so your life.

ld.

The only way to get
anything done is to
start to do it, really
keep on focusing your
energies on you'll do
that it, understanding
that you're going you
going to be great at
everything. And
then relax.

Langston Hughes

Pick the places you want to be great at and that you really want to focus your energies on and do that, understanding that you're not going to be great at everything. And then relax.

Ursula Burns

If I believe I am the person I want to become,
it just gets done.

Lana del Rey

If you want something hard enough, it just gets done.

Billy Strayhorn

I'm sick of following my dreams, I'm just going to ask them where they're going, and hook up with them later.

Mitch Hedburg

Truth always originates
in a minority of one,
and every custom
begins as a broken
precedent.

...up with
them later.

Will J. Durant

change the world.

change the world.

Barack Obama

We can't just sit
around wringing
our hands. We
need to recover
from the shock
to step... of
and history and
move... so that we
always done in this
country.... We need
to get to work.

Oprah Winfrey

We can't just sit around wringing our hands. We need to recover from our shock and depression and do what we have always done in this country.... We need to get to work.

Michelle Obama

Josephine Baker

ve. of a
y. You can't
sordidife.
ld.

Barbara Grizzuti Harrison

Joan Harris (*Mad Men*)

When you have exhausted all possibilities, "remember this — you haven't."

Thomas Edison

When you have exhausted all possibilities, remember this— you haven't.

David Bowie

Whenever I dwell for any length of time on my own shortcomings, they gradually begin to seem mild, harmless, rather engaging little things, not at all like the staring defects in other people's characters. You've got to search for it.

Margaret Halsey

Heundiffyisltotingyis
fortteynrallygotthrough
bdwlifeoaadthnugh
ofitdaysaamdyowdon't
skpotronolgistht's a
yenyusalylebegingto
sexporirinid, (bliss)less,
Anttdocongapgodtktow
thowgo, dottaalslike
tonethringdefeetoin
ddh'r jestsismble
abross.Yu've got to
search for it.

George Harrison

Because you are
alive, everything
is possible.

possible.

Thich Nhat Hanh

When nothing
is sure,
everything is
possible.

Margaret Drabble

My ambition is to
enjoy my life and to do
exactly what I want to
do. And I'll do that.
I will be free.

Venus Williams

My ambition is to
engage everywhere,
exactly what I cannot
be denied.

Your task is to
enjoy life everywhere, do
exactly what I want to
do. And I'll do that.
I will be free.

Millicent Garrett

Joan of Arc went
into battle
saying to her
troops "I am not
going to begin
it serenely see if
you're following
spirit I'm going to
remembered Course
all the men had to
run after her.

Ingrid Bergman

Finish each day
and be done with
it. Tomorrow
is a new day.
You shall begin
it serenely and
with too high a
spirit to be
encumbered
with your old
nonsense.

Ralph Waldo Emerson

Don't loaf and invite
inspiration; light out
after it with a
club.

Jack London

If you're offered a seat
on a rocket ship, don't
ask what seat.
Just get on.

Sheryl Sandberg

Go for it.